JoJo Siwa
THINGS I LOVE

A FILL-IN FRIENDSHIP JOURNAL

AMULET BOOKS
NEW YORK

nickelodeon

DO YOU KNOW ANY OTHER SIWANATORZ? HOW HAVE THE SIWANATORZ HELPED YOU FIND FRIENDS?

Share online with #SiwanatorzRule!

....
....
....
....
....
....
....
....
....
....
....
....
....
....

IF YOUR BEST FRIEND WERE AN ANIMAL, WHAT WOULD SHE BE? WHAT WOULD YOU BE?

I have two best friends, Halle and Jayna. All three of us would be monkeys. monkeys are really cool, and being a monkey would be fun! We'd play on the playground and have fun together, and it would be great.

Xo, JoJo

PASTE A NOTE FROM A FRIEND IN THE SPACE BELOW! HOW DID GETTING THE NOTE MAKE YOU FEEL?

BFF: 4 YOUR 👁👁 ONLY

ASK YOUR FRIENDS WHAT THEY LOVE MOST ABOUT YOU! WHICH ANSWERS, IF ANY, SURPRISED YOU?

....

....

....

....

....

....

....

....

....

....

....

....

....

....

WHAT IS A FUN MEMORY YOU SHARE WITH YOUR FRIENDS FROM SCHOOL?

List below and online with #BookWormz!

....
....
....
....
....
....
....
....
....
....
....
....
....
....

DO YOU PREFER TO HAVE A LOT OF FRIENDS OR JUST A FEW CLOSE FRIENDS? EXPLAIN WHY.

FRIENDS CAN BE ANYWHERE!
WHERE HAVE YOU FOUND AN UNEXPECTED FRIEND?

HOW DO YOU SHOW LOVE
TO YOUR FRIENDS?

DESCRIBE YOUR PERFECT DAY.
WHAT WOULD YOU DO? WHERE WOULD YOU GO, IF YOU COULD GO ANYWHERE? WHO WOULD BE THERE?

A TRUE FRIEND IS . . .
COMPLETE THE SENTENCE.

....

....

....

....

....

....

....

....

....

....

....

....

....

CAN YOU DESCRIBE ONE TIME THAT A FRIEND CAME TO YOUR RESCUE?

....
....
....
....
....
....
....
....
....
....
....
....
....
....

CAN YOU REMEMBER A TIME THAT SOMEONE WAS MEAN TO YOU? DID YOUR FRIENDS HAVE YOUR BACK?

Share below and on social media with #PeaceOutHaterz!

....

....

....

....

....

....

....

....

....

....

....

....

....

MINI YEARBOOK:

USE THESE PAGES TO DOODLE AND TO EXCHANGE NOTES WITH A FRIEND.

**Write down your hopes for
each other in the coming year!**

WHAT IS A FAVORITE SUMMER MEMORY THAT YOU HAVE WITH YOUR BEST FRIEND?

....

....

....

....

....

....

....

....

....

....

....

....

....

....

HAVE YOU EVER FOUGHT WITH A FRIEND? HOW DID YOU SOLVE THE PROBLEM?

....
....
....
....
....
....
....
....
....
....
....
....
....
....

WHAT YEAR OF YOUR LIFE HAVE YOU LOVED THE MOST? WHAT MADE THAT YEAR GREAT?

I think 2017 was my favorite year of my life. 2017 was

unbelievable! So much happened—I got signed with

Nickelodeon, I did my own TV special, my book came out,

my new music videos were released, and I just did a lot

of fun things!

Xo, JoJo

JOJO HAS FRIENDS IN OMAHA AND LOS ANGELES. DO YOU HAVE A FRIEND WHO LIVES FAR AWAY? HOW DO YOU KEEP IN TOUCH?

....

....

....

....

....

....

....

....

....

....

....

....

....

....

....

....

....

GRAB A FRIEND AND DESIGN BUMPER STICKERS FOR YOUR BIKES IN THE SPACE BELOW. WHAT WOULD YOUR MATCHING BUMPER STICKERS LOOK LIKE?

WHEN JOJO WAS A LITTLE GIRL, SHE DREAMED OF BEING A POP STAR. IMAGINE YOU AND A FRIEND TEN YEARS FROM NOW. WHAT WILL YOU EACH BE LIKE? WHERE WILL YOU LIVE, AND WHAT WILL YOU DO PROFESSIONALLY?

....

....

....

....

....

....

....

....

....

....

....

WRITE DOWN QUALITIES THAT CORRESPOND WITH THE LETTERS OF A FRIEND'S NAME!

For example, **LIZ** = Lucky, Interesting, Zany.

....

....

....

....

....

....

....

....

....

....

....

....

....

....

....

....

WHAT IS YOUR FAVORITE MOVIE ABOUT FRIENDSHIP? WHAT DID IT TEACH YOU?

One of my favorite movies ever
is Elf. I love it because the big elf
is friends with the little brother,
and I think that's really cute!

Xo, JoJo

JOJO AND HER BIG BROTHER ARE BEST FRIENDS. THEY LOVE TO GO SWIMMING, TO AMUSEMENT PARKS, AND TO ESCAPE ROOMS. WHAT DO YOU DO WITH YOUR RELATIVES THAT BRINGS YOU CLOSER?

Share online with #FamilyMatters!

....

....

....

....

....

....

....

....

....

....

....

....

....

DO YOU HAVE AN ANIMAL FRIEND? WHAT IS HIS OR HER NAME?

....

....

....

....

....

....

....

....

....

....

....

....

....

DRAW A PICTURE OF YOUR FAVORITE PLACE IN THE WORLD.

WHAT ARE YOUR FAVORITE ACTIVITIES TO DO WITH YOUR FRIENDS?

Share online with #CantStopWontStop!

....

....

....

....

....

....

....

....

....

....

....

....

....

....

HOW DO YOU MAKE NEW FRIENDS? WRITE DOWN THREE STRATEGIES YOU BELIEVE IN! (For example, "Say 'hello' first.")

....

....

....

....

....

....

....

....

....

....

....

....

....

....

....

....

WHAT IS THE LAST SILLY THING YOU DID WITH A FRIEND?

 The one thing we do when we're together every single time is play Monopoly! We have to do it every time we have a sleepover. We love the game, but we make up our own rules. ☺

XO, JoJo

JOJO LOVES SCARY THINGS, ESPECIALLY HAUNTED HOUSES! WHAT SCARY STORIES DO YOU LOVE?

....
....
....
....
....
....
....
....
....
....
....
....
....
....

WHAT IS A FAVORITE CANDY AMONG YOU AND YOUR FRIENDS?

....

....

....

....

....

....

....

....

....

....

....

....

....

....

JOJO'S CLOSET IS FULL OF SNEAKERS IN ALL DIFFERENT COLORS! WHAT ACCESSORIES DO YOU LOVE THE MOST?

....

....

....

....

....

....

....

....

....

....

....

....

....

....

WHO IS YOUR NEWEST FRIEND?
HOW DID YOU MEET?

Share online with #FriendsAreEverywhere!

My newest friend is a girl on Nickelodeon: Breanna Yde

from School of Rock. She's an awesome friend, and

we're the same age. We talk and FaceTime all the time!

Xo, JoJo

A HAIKU IS A POEM THAT HAS THREE LINES WITH FIVE SYLLABLES IN THE FIRST LINE, SEVEN IN THE SECOND, AND FIVE IN THE THIRD.
WRITE A HAIKU ABOUT A FRIEND.
NOW SET IT TO MUSIC!

....

....

....

....

....

....

....

....

....

....

....

....

DO YOU AND YOUR FRIENDS KEEP ONE ANOTHER'S SECRETS? WHAT KIND OF SECRETS ARE THE HARDEST TO KEEP?

HAVE YOU EVER FORMED A CLUB? IF
SO, WRITE THE CLUB NAME BELOW!
IF NOT, USE THIS SPACE TO MAKE AN
IMAGINARY CLUB AND TO SET
CLUB RULES!

....
....
....
....
....
....
....
....
....
....
....
....
....

JOJO PLAYED CATCHER FOR HER SOFTBALL
TEAM WHEN SHE WAS YOUNGER. DO YOU
OR YOUR FRIENDS PLAY SPORTS OR
ANY OTHER SCHOOL ACTIVITY? HOW
HAS SHARING AN INTEREST BROUGHT
YOU TOGETHER?

JOJO AND HER MOM HAVE CODE WORDS FOR EACH OTHER, BASED ON THEIR BEST FRIENDS' NAMES (KIM AND HALLE!). NICKNAMES = LOVE.
WHAT NICKNAMES DO YOU AND YOUR FRIENDS HAVE FOR ONE ANOTHER? COME UP WITH A NEW ONE FOR YOUR BFF AND HAVE HER DO THE SAME!

....
....
....
....
....
....
....
....
....
....

WHO'S YOUR CELEBRITY FRIEND-CRUSH? SAY WHY!

If I could pick a celebrity to be best friends with, I would
say it would be Meghan Trainor—she's really cool. ☺
                        Xo, JoJo

PLAY "TRUTH OR DANCE" WITH A FRIEND! TELL EACH OTHER A SECRET OR MAKE UP A DANCE!

DESCRIBE A TIME WHEN A FRIEND HAS SURPRISED YOU!

....

....

....

....

....

....

....

....

....

....

....

....

....

WHO WOULD PLAY YOUR GIRL CREW IN A MOVIE ABOUT YOUR LIVES?

I'd have my real friends in my girl crew: Breanna, Jayna,
Halle, my mom, and my dog!

Xo, JoJo

WHAT SONG BEST DESCRIBES YOU AND YOUR FRIENDS? Share online with #JoJosJamz!

It would have to be "California Gurls" by Katy Perry—
even though we're not all from California!

XO, JoJo

....

....

....

....

....

....

....

....

....

....

....

....

....

....

....

....

....

....

WHICH HOLIDAY DO YOU LOVE THE MOST, AND WHY?

....
....
....
....
....
....
....
....
....
....
....
....
....

DO YOU AND YOUR FRIENDS HAVE
MATCHING T-SHIRTS OR BRACELETS
THAT REPRESENT YOUR FRIENDSHIP?
DRAW THEM IN A PICTURE BELOW!
IF YOU DON'T HAVE SOMETHING LIKE
THAT ALREADY, GET A PARENT TO HELP
YOU DECORATE OLD T-SHIRTS WITH
MATCHING PUFFY PAINT DOODLES!

IF YOU AND YOUR FRIENDS COULD SWAP PLACES WITH ANYONE ELSE IN THE WORLD, WHO WOULD YOU CHOOSE, AND WHY?

Share your answers with #FriendSwap!

....

....

....

....

....

....

....

....

....

....

....

....

....

....

BEING A SIWANATOR MEANS BEING KIND. HOW DO YOU AND YOUR FRIENDS TREAT OTHER KIDS WITH KINDNESS?